WILDHUNDREDS

PITT POETRY SERIES

Ed Ochester, Editor

WILDHUNDREDS

NATE MARSHALL
UNIVERSITY OF PITTSBURGH PRESS

Published by the University of Pittsburgh Press, Pittsburgh, Pa., 15260
Copyright © 2015, Nate Marshall
All rights reserved
Manufactured in the United States of America
Printed on acid-free paper
10 9 8 7 6 5 4 3 2 1
ISBN 13: 978-0-8229-6383-7
ISBN 10: 0-8229-6383-3

This book is for my grandparents (Eola & James Sr., Mickey & Mae Frances), for bringing us to the Hundreds and teaching us how to make home in a new place.

•

To the victims of state-supported and -sanctioned black death, from Emmitt Till to Damo Franklin to Rekia Boyd. Our lives matter. Y'all still live 'cause we still live & write & fight.

CONTENTS

i.

ii.

iii.

i.

you don't ever leave home. you take your home with you.
you better . . . otherwise you're homeless.

—James Baldwin

repetition & repetition &

ours is a long love song,
a push out into open air,
a stare into the barrel,
a pool of grief puddling
under our single body.
a national shame
amnesia & shame again.
we are a pattern,
a percussive imperative,
a break beat.
we are live
on the airwaves,
until they close,
in the pubs
until they close,
in the schools
until they close.
we are close
to the edge of the city limits.
we are limited to the hood
until we decide we are not.

baby we are hundreds:
wild until we are free.
wild like amnesia
& shame,
amnesia until
we realize that it's
crazy to keep forgetting
& we ain't crazy
baby we are wild.
we are 1.
we are love.

pronounce

wild hundreds

starts with a tire's squeal
at getaway. broken whistle
of the coffee kettle
because work is waiting.
while.

next part is a clan, a wild
bunch on the outskirts of civil.
the name she calls you
when she loves you casually.
hun.

the end, a beginning.
what we say when we name
ourselves. a dropped
letter to save time.
its.

wildhundreds
wilhundreds
wilhundeds
whilehunits.

Fame Food & Liquor

we cut down 115th street for a quicker stroll
past the pastor's house, vacant lot, liquor store.

buses pointing out the hood & back. the route
every morning goes by the liquor store.

the loose Philly blunts hard & dry. the sour mouth
washed away by a dull gulp of liquor. store

a honey bun in your fat back pocket. pray
nobody notices your awkward walk. this liquor store

sees stumbling often. out front the garish stickers fluoresce
on the wire windows like winos with liquor store

bottles. a small weapon sits behind the counter hidden by the cigarettes
& candy small enough to steal. when the liquor store

is locked up the rolling metals make the window
a pastoral, part of our natural habitat. behold the liquor store:

the sugar waters, the Ziploc bag of coins
& Nate's tongue the color of loose pennies in the liquor store.

god made the hundreds, man made it wild

they mama tell them it wild over there she say over there buses
quit running like utilities or dead boys in them hundreds they
schools lock doors after the tardy bell like prison standards is low
like the waistline of uniform pants dropout rates is high dropouts
is high like them girls shorts come the month of May for them
police officers is hall monitors them businesses over there fail like
the schools most all fail except liquor stores, them never close
over there them streets burning them blocks hot them people
fired it wild them police over there is overworked & not working
they don't got enough of them police they do got too busy sitting
in Walgreens parking lot hiding from the fire

Harold's Chicken Shack #1

i was born by a lake, chicken shack,
& a church
— Common, "The Morning"

1st defense against food deserts.
when the whitefolk wouldn't sling
us burgers you gave no fuck.
stuck your golden-ringed hand
into the flour & fixed the bird.

you 1st example of black flight.
original innovation of deep fry.
you beef tallow, city slick
& down home migration taste.

of course your sauce sweet
& burn at the same time.
of course you call it mild
so whitefolk won't know
to fear until it's too late.

you no corporate structure,
just black business
model. they earn the recipe
& go make it their own.

every cut of crow you
throw in the grease is dark
meat. the whole shack:
shaking, drenched in mild
sauce, sweet spirit, baptized.

Granddaddy was the neighborhood

1.

he moved deep South Side in the sixties
when whitefolk was still there.
Mama was a girl & Peoria Street
was Polack & I-talian & Jew.

                                   & Granddaddy
was a home owner & a black man
on an odd block until every block
became black once the whitefolk
left like broken fever & blackfolk brought
their claustrophobia out to the hundreds
for a single family home & a lawn & park.

he became a mailman in Beverly Hills, Chicago
& the whitefolk there loved him like a man
who worked   for them   cause he did

2.

there's gaps   something
about gin,   another thing about
fucking up   property,   people,
other loves,   just fucking   leaving Grandma
& the house   for a condo & a daughter-aged
woman.

somewhere   there was his father
         who beat   the shit out of   wife & daughter
                 maybe called
his son a sissy   or something like that

3.

there's a grandson
with Granddaddy's name,
a gut to follow & fill.
Granddaddy, all Dobbs hats & boxing gloves,
hypothetical slick talk to girls & stumble
from the bar's cologne & his.
Granddaddy all leisure suits & peppermint.
Granddaddy all birthday money & slurry speech
Granddaddy all Grandma kicking him out
but he still Granddaddy

& he still all the stories & all the gaps
& every block in the hood
working.

buying new shoes

he sees the Nikes
boxed, beautiful,
hundred plus. he
hopes. he holds
the box under his
arm like a briefcase
for the unfortunate
business of being
told no.

Chicago high school love letters

first day of school

1.

i would take the bus
to you, walk through
your neighborhood
& navigate the colors.

3.

take my student ID.
it's clipped
in the corner for
             free lunch.

out south

> . . . *And they, since they*
> *were not the one dead, turned to their affairs.*
> — Robert Frost, "Out, Out"

in Chicago kids are beaten. they crack
open; they're pavement. they don't fight, they die.
bodies bruised blue with wood. cameras catch
us killing, capture danger to broadcast

on Broadways. we Roseland stars made players
for the press. apes caged from 1st grade until.
shake us. we make terrible tambourines.
packed into class, kids passed like kidney stones.

each street day is unanswered prayer for peace,
news gushes from Mom's mouth like schoolboy blood.
Ragtown crime don't stop, only waves—hello.
crime waves break no surface on news—goodbye.

every kid that's killed is one less free lunch,
a fiscal coup. welcome to where we from.

palindrome

after Lisel Mueller

on her profile i see she has 2 kids,
now 1 she had in high school, now none
at all. she unaborts 1.
she is unpregnant
in 8th grade. she unresembles
her favorite pop singer Pink. she uncuts
her hair, it pulls into her scalp from clumps on the floor.
her new boyfriend forgets the weight of her.
she leaves her new boyfriend. he's forgetting
her phone number. she becomes my girlfriend
she picks up the phone & i am on the line
ungiving a goodbye. her best friend trades letters
between us. we each open letters
from ourselves with hearts on the outside.
she transfers to our magnet school. she moves
to a neighborhood close by. we separate
at the lips. we have never kissed behind the school.
she unchecks the yes box on the note & i take away
my middle school love letter. i unmeet her cop father
& her Chicano moms. we walk backward into Baskin-Robbins
throwing up gold medal ribbon ice cream into cups.
it rounds into scoops, flattens into gallon drums
of sugar & cream & coldness. we are six years old.
maybe we can go back to then. i unlearn
her name, the way it is spelled the same
backward. how it flips on a page, or in my mouth.
i never knew words could do that
until 5 minutes from now.

Foot Locker

Evanston, IL

the sales associate has no idea about my size.
he spies from the top of a ladder, no pretension

of acting like he was reaching for the fitted hat. the other
associate at ground level, close to my spine

as the off-brand backpack i wear.
i think about buying a new piece of cool

with the summer camp savings my mom
has 10 monthed into a plastic bag of travelers' checks

but i can't breathe enough suburb
to be frivolous so i walk out. later

a white kid in my camp group shows me the guts of his bookbag
stuffed full with hats, headbands, t-shirts.

1st love song to the black girl at smart camp

you are all
the white
girls' cute
in just you.

your color,
1 lovely freckle,
unending, unerring,
the right brown.

even before i saw you
every kid on campus
sung your song
to me: *she is your*

type, your kind
of girl, you like
it like how
she is.

niggaicouldhavebeen #1

when we moved back to Chicago
i couldn't code switch
'til almost high school.

my sister picked up
South Side slang
like dice on concrete.

if i learned
to slur earlier
i might not have

been tertium quid of niggerdom.
might have been jumped in,
not jumped.

candy store

on the front porch
or in a basement kitchen
a sour pickle
fat as a child's forearm
with a peppermint stick
stuffed in the middle
sits inside a jar.

plastic sandwich bag jammed
with Frooties or Tootsies.

past-prime Sour Patch Kids
or fruit chews sticky &
stubborn to the chew.

a piece of hard candy
on a ring & wrapped
in plastic ready to hand
to that neighbor's cousin
with the light eyes &
white teeth.

salt & sour chips
or the dill flavor
in the bright green bag.

fluorescent barrel juices
with foil tops.

Flamin' Hot Cheetos
turn tongues & fingers
Michael Jordan jersey
red for the rest of the day.

2 crock pots:
orange-yellow bubble of cheese sauce,
dirt brown of ground beef
ready for heat.

Chicago high school love letters

homecoming weekend

46.

come to the dance.
my hands wand
around your frame
searching for danger.

58.

you can wear my letterman jacket
home. if it's the wrong shade
of blue imagine it around
you while it sits in your locker.

the break

is the place in the funk record
everybody goes crazy. if the dj is smart
the break is built longer. the break is hip-hop.

Grandmaster Flash took the break,
stretched the break. pulled it apart
like silly putty, plastered the party in it.

the break is where the drums take center
stage. the break is the center. the break
is the party. the break is built
from thrown-out equipment,
unused grooves. the break is struggle.

the break is the place
your sister doesn't have.
the break is the eviction.
the break is moving
back in with Moms.

the break is the break-
up. the break is garbage
bags of your sister's
belongings you find
in your room the day you
come back from summer camp.

the break is the party
you want to have
for your sister. the break
is your sister not being
only yours anymore.

your niece is the break.
the job applications
are the break. listening
to Lil' Kim & Biggie
while your sister braids
your niece's hair is the break.

the break is the job
your sister hates.

the break is the apartment hunt.
the arguments between Moms
& your sister. the break,
the apartment coming through.
the break, garbage bags
absent from your room.

Harold's Chicken Shack #35

fried gizzards w/ fries

your dad orders it for you
& you are too young
to know what you'll have
to swallow &
too old to refuse food.

good sauce is equality
for all fowl. you know
this crunch & thickness
around your tongue.

what changes is texture.
gizzard is stubborn,
muscular. you grind your
teeth like nervous sleep
to eat. you push all the hard
down your throat, away
from your taste buds.

gizzard is a bird's first
stomach to help
the avian break down
what it consumes.

you too swallow difficult shit
like gizzards & if
you're lucky sauce
might help. & if you're not
praise anyway. gravel
is necessary food.

learning gang handshakes

after Lucille Clifton

my 1 hand holding tight
to the neighborhood, stubborn
& still. this hand has never been
crooked, never cradled the love
or hate side of a pistol, never punched
with no regret. my hand is small,
hairless as a newborn. my wrist, thin as a promise
breaking. this is shaking up in the park.
the big boys have deemed me not soft
today. they see the way
i ball, a blur & menace. wild
as a punch landed in the wrong stomach
or a bullet through the big
picture window, lodged into a living
room wall. i dive into concrete
for the loose ball, stroke heavy at arms, swim
in a pool of blood that we still won't call
a personal foul. have you played a pickup game
running red from 3 distinct places on your person? if not
then don't throw up any sign of the South Side.
when the big boys taught me how to hug with palms
i learned the secret. shaking up looks like violence
& love. & it is. the fingers at the end
freeze in a pose like sutra, bent, only an inch away
from breaking. both partners in the dance of hands know
they could crush the knuckle of the other.
they know *all is 1*, they whisper
this fusion in mean mug
my other hand; come celebrate.

hood woods

from the woods raccoons,
squirrels, rabbits, possums,
rats ran together like teammates.

the trees clumped menacing
as a group of big boys until smoke
started to pour toward the park on our block.

we heard our mothers best
white voices rattle alarm into the telephone.
every kid & old folk perched on porches,

watched the black smoke swallow the neighborhood
like blackfolk did 40 years ago. the temperature raised
& we took off our windbreakers, saw orange lick

up tree trunks, we thought we felt rain & all us kids danced
until we noticed our shirts fading, our hair graying
from what burning rained over us.

ii.

turns out if you don't die you just keep getting older.

— Angel Nafis

Mama says

1.

    you gotta go to the head dr.
says all this brooding is gonna kill
you or her or somebody. all this kill
in you & your temper short & you

ready to firecracker at the slightest.
this ain't healthy she say. you fight
her wish. you fine you say. fine as
everybody else. you just 16 & man

in progress & in the process of
hardening into survivor. but she pull
rank on you. talk to the doc or quit
the basketball team. & man ain't

man in Chi with no ball so you bend.
at the shrink there's a head test.
it ask you about fire & fantasizing
about burning or murder or hearing

voices or rape & other synonyms.
& you know the right answers have
to be the ones that ain't crazy.
& that is crazy because a sick

person wouldn't be able to decipher
sickness on the scantron. & you
talk to the shrink & he's a nice
old white guy & you're not

really talking about much but he's
okay so you don't feel as bad
going back the second time.

2.

when Michelle Obama was
asked about her fear of racists
killing her husband now that he
was running for president

she says *he's a black man*
on the South Side. he can die
any day. at the gas station
or grocery store.

the shrink suspects you are
learning the same lesson.

3.

he diagnoses you with fear
'cause your boy down the block

just got smacked baseball bat
to his temple & the homie
you used to play ball with at
the park got shot the year before

                                                etc. etc. . . .

& that's something you gotta
adjust to. get used to: this body
dropping rhythm, blood percussion,
heart beats hitting b-boy freeze.

the shrink is nice about it & says
you're clear & don't have to come
back.

4.

you quit basketball that year
because tryouts is the same day

Granny dies from cancer.
at the funeral you don't cry.
you're clear. you're fine.
there's nothing wrong.

Ragtown prayer

for Tyrone Lawson

1.

Dear Heavenly Father
As we gather 2ma wit broken
hearts, lost souls, & heavy
emotions to bury our love
1 Tyrone we ask that you give
us strength. We kno he's in
a better place watching down
on us & you never make mistakes.

I'm askn you watch over Tyrone's
family & Us . . . his Ragtown family.
A lot of us dnt come 2 you
bt that's tha best thing about family . . .
1 prayer can cover us all!!! We love
& miss you Tyrone!

R.I.P / B.I.P AMEN
FROM ME & RAGTOWN

2.

No Father (Maybe He Heavenly?).
2ma is broken. what we gather
from this heavy life is souls, hearts,
buried emotions, our love (& brother
Tyrone is 1). you give, took him, no ask.
We strength, he kno us.
Better places watching down
on us mistakes. You make nevers.

I'm over you. Tyrone askn
Us . . . *family? Family? & Ragtown?*
2 a lot of us it is
family: that best thing, tha
cover, 1 prayer, love,
Tyrone, a miss, & you.

MEN & ME
A RAGTOWN
R.I.P.

Note: The 1st section was a Facebook
status on the eve of Tyrone's funeral.

in the land where whitefolk jog

he walk down the road
dark & abandoned
skullcap & scowl
quick stride & limp.
he mug & bump
the sound of *fuck you up*
in his headphones.
he hear what goes bump
other than him in the new
moon's no light. he brace
for everything. he slide
his key in between
2 fingers of his fist
readies to aim somewhere
soft & exposed.
he contemplates a cheek
or eye socket.

he raise his hand out of pocket
like a holster & cocks elbow.
& the pat pat of New Balances
bounce down & around the
corner. & she glows in her
peach thigh & sunflower
shorts & she pat pat &
he remembers key between fingers
is for locking & also entry.

he enters a decade earlier
hoping for glory
to wash him in high school.
he straps up high-top only
athletic shoe he owns & is off.

he around the corner & over the glitter
of exploded Wild Irish Roses. he thump
thump & crosses the paths of pits
& shepherds & rottweilers.

he see the neighborhood people there
& he thump thump & they do too.
he know they never seen someone run
in not their hardest way.
he never ran in less.

he never been in land where
jog is a memory.
he never knew someone to run
without having to join them
or stop them in their tracks.

Chicago high school love letters

131.

i would
airbrush
you on
a t-shirt.

156.

i would fight for you
like my shoes or my
boys or any excuse
for contact.

landing

surprise escapes your lips as you soar
into the sinking of having your shins
kicked from under you. if you're lucky
the full nelson that folds arms origami
will keep your knees from crashing
into the concrete. your flight will be
brief. pray you have enough time
to kick back into the kneecap
of the 3rd assailant. if the 4th member
of the crew sees your retaliation,
it's a toss-up. he might be merciful,
dock his Nikes into your stomach,
ribs, knees, & not face, head, spine. he might
not be merciful. hopefully the other 3 guys
will only tap-dance on your hands, break
something that might heal. if a car stops,
you'll make it. the driver isn't on their side,
this time. this time, you'll only miss 1 day
of school for the emergency room visit,
the negative x-rays, the scratched retina,
the doctor's orders, the protective eyewear.
this time 5 years from now you will miss
all of this. the beauty of soaring,
or being sore.

Alzheimer's

. . . I have seen the gunman kill and go free to kill again.
Carl Sandburg, "Chicago"

my nephew doesn't know his address.
my granddad can't remember his childhood
address. i find it in a scrapbook,
a Western Union message to his mom
from his Navy days.   *4328 S. Greenwood.*
the Black Belt. Trayvon's killer walked free tonight.
i went to the old address & cried in my car.
this is where i came from.

i drive away & remember Keller Gifted School.
i head south on i-94 & then west toward
the school. it sits in the Mount Greenwood neighborhood.
Mount Greenwood was white & scary. in 4th grade
the neighborhood kids would piss on our playground,
break windows, scrawl *NIGGER* on the walls outside.

the neighborhood parents knew. the neighborhood
parents were busy burning
the newly black-owned house down the block.
this is where i came from. whitefolk
violence isn't hypothetical to me. it's not historical
or systemic. its elementary school
like Pokémon or sleepovers.

My granddad can't remember where
he grew up. i can. my nephew doesn't
know his address yet. he'll remember it soon.

on being called a nigger in Ann Arbor, MI, on South University Street by a drunk ticket scalper

the quick simmer
the immediate
boil under skin
the tighten of
fingers into fist
there is a rush
of blood
i fantasize
about turning back
to meet the
white boy where
he sits on the concrete
& use the wall
behind for leverage
as i mudhole
into his neck.

there's the swing
back away from
his direction
when my second
mind takes over.

i punch my fist
so hard into
my hand it aches
for hours my face
clenches & i
can feel the tears
just underneath
another ecstasy
i won't allow
myself today.

Chicago high school love letters

spring break

214.

i know all the museum
free days by heart. you
the exhibit i steal touch
from in shadow.

226.

i'll stay with you.
even after
the streetlights come
on or don't.

prelude

he must've moved out
the neighborhood when i was little.
i bet he could ball,
probably could dunk.

                        maybe he rap now.

maybe he is the boy on every wall.

we ain't got graffiti over here
like for real art stuff but maybe
in the '80s he was optimistic. this was his all
city attempt all over the hood.

maybe he ain't a he.

in the time before the Folks
Nation ran everything over here
maybe the presiding clique was RIP.

i see it everywhere:

        RIP Pierre
        RIP Bird
        RIP D
        RIP Man Man

maybe RIP is a girl.
i see her name next to all
the bad boys. all the big boys
my mama told me not to fool with.
maybe she's all they girlfriends
at once. but they all
gone. no wonder
she keep finding new boys
to kiss.

39

Indian summer

heat is a cruel mother,
        pushes us out into the neighborhood
        to play & burn. the sun sit up top
        like an OG on a tall stoop
        fresh out from Stateville,
        nervous around 4 walls.
        the clouds circle vulture
        or blunt session or after-school fight
        above. we out here
        playing with 1 ear
        gaping, both eyes low. summertime
        & dying is easier. june is jazz
        or a funeral dirge. july, thick thump
        of a rap record or dull thud of
        hood cliché. the weatherman says
        forecast is clear, beautiful, &
        sunny. that's a cloud in our sky.
        your play cousin got good hair,
        Indian in her family. maybe
        she can pray for rain.

when it comes back

in the locker room
i'm staring at the far wall fresh
off the weights considering the treadmill
or just dressing & going. a white boy is
naked in my sight line

& mumbling:
        . . . get dressed & go . . .
                        . . . hanging around . . .
    . . . fucking queer . . .

i don't know if I hear him right   so I stop thinking
about the treadmill. i hold my hoodie, hoist it
over my head & down across my frame.
the white boy (who is my daddy's age)
repeats himself & won't put a towel over his waist.
his stomach is an ugly puff of cloud above his cock
& he keeps talking
in a lover's tone:
        . . . go home . . .
    . . . damn fairy . . .

i'm back at Pullman Park.
i'm a boy again with a brick
in my hand, a boy under me. my brick
kisses the boy in his mouth & i'm on top
of the boy. my hand
becoming the brick.

meanwhile i make out
the word   *f_ggot.*

the white boy might be a veteran,
an untreated mental health case to be so mad
at someone for sitting in a public place
& i'm some kind of veteran untreated mental health
case. we're closer than he knows.
doesn't he know that i could fuck   him   up
if i wanted to? i'm fresh off the hack squat machine,
my legs are coiled
                              & i could kill him.

pallbearers

The ones that hold you when you can't really stand. That's crew . . .
Ang 13, "My Crew"

Dom, Kenny, Shaun, Bart, & i were close as a coffin.
promised we would always be tight.
we made it to every middle school dance.
weaving through crowds of kids we kept moving
behind a nervous girl's hips, mesmerized by the split
of skirts & smiles at our request. we didn't know much.

in those days we never had much
we threw our pennies like roses on a coffin
into PlayStation games to split.
even when money was tight
we could cop a 5-dollar pizza, keep it moving,
everybody got a slice. this was the dance

of being best friends. teaching Bart to dance
like a black boy. Bart forgetting how much
the Polish heirloom i broke cost. helping Shaun make moving
on from old girlfriends easier. Shaun & me moving the coffin
of my dj's turntables. us getting Kenny's jump shot tight.
playing for money, only to take the winnings & split

them on bus fare. the day Shaun's pants split
in school we told him to dance
around until we found replacements that weren't too tight.
we laughed but helped him avoid too much
embarrassment. we covered for him like a closed coffin.
told him watch the way he was moving.

i remember Kenny moving
to Dom's neighborhood when his parents split.
the way he spoke about his father cold, a coffin.
we comforted him, me & Shaun showed him how to dance
through single-parent life. we knew there was so much
change in our lives. but we held to each other tight.

last summer our time was tight
& we only got together once before moving
away. since 1st semester Shaun & Bart don't talk much
to Kenny. Dom hasn't been around since he split
to work with kids in New Orleans. i've been learning to dance
like corporate interns do. my cubicle is quiet as a coffin.

but i remember my chest tight, Grandma not moving.
that day my crew was much closer than anyone could split
when she was done with life's dance & in a coffin.

Chicago high school love letters

prom weekend

320.

jump the broom
or turnstile. no car
except kiss. no ride
except want.

331.

this song is dedicated
to you: either R. Kelly
or R. Kelly. love
ballad or elegy.

praise song

praise the Hennessy, the brown
shine, the dull burn. praise
the dare, the *take it*, the no face
you're supposed to make.
praise the house, its many rooms,
hardwood & butter leather couches
its richness. praise the rich, their friendship.
praise the friends: the child of the well-off,
the child of the well-off, the child of well
the child of welfare, the child of welfare.
praise the diversity but praise the Hennessy,
& again,   & again.   praise
the new year upon us. praise my stumble,
the shaky eye, the fluid arm, but the steady
hand. praise my hand, the burning it has,
praise the dive into the gut of a friend, the dousing
of my hand in his ribs, praise the softness of skin,
the way it always gives.

praise the pulling, the calming down.

praise the *fuck that*, the jump back into all
5 of my friends fist first. praise all
5 of my friends pinning me into the thick
carpet, knees in my back, praise my back
how it hurts & raises anyway how it flips,
how it's the best friend of my fists.
praise the swinging pool cue, how it whips
air like a disobedient child. praise the disobedient
& all the chilling   i won't do.
praise the child smile on my face, the fun
plunging a knee into a cheek of my best friend.
praise his blood, the brightness of it, a sun i bask in.

praise my blood, the nose flowing wild with effort,
the mess & taste of it, praise the swallowing,
salt & its sweetness.

praise the morning, the impossible blue,
midwestern January above us, praise
the blues dulled in my denim by all
the brown, praise the brown shine, the dull
burn.

praise all 6 in my jeans, our salt
& life sitting dry on my thighs
mixing, refusing to wash away.

iii.

. . . once you've come to be part of this particular patch,
you'll never love another. like loving a woman with a broken
nose, you may well find lovelier lovelies. but never a lovely so real.

— Nelson Algren, "Chicago: City on the Make"

the last graduation

in the voice of an 8th-grade graduate

get home & take off the gown.
fold it perfect, put it in a plastic sleeve.
sit the hat on top, watch the golden tassel fan out
like a pond struck by a skipping stone.

tuck away the fake snakeskin shoes
& the polyester pantsuit.
reach for the Sox fitted.

>   it is crumpled;
>   a dull, deep black
>   we learn to be.

shrug out of the house
in high top FILAs
ready to throw rock.
head for the asphalt
pond, skipping
stones in hand.
ready to make waves.

the first graduation

in the voice of another 8th-grade graduate

no cap or gown, just a suit,
collar unbuttoned, a cap toe.

ceremony is mere reception,
no worry. there will be other
moments to capture.

       when my parents try to take a picture
       i pitch a fit, spit their names in the air
       demand we leave this perfectly
       maintained middle school auditorium.

slide out of the dress clothes.
leave them for the help to fold. reach
for my tattered Cubs hat, the ease
that there will be other hats to wear.
bike to the park, summer baseball
to play. there are throws to make
& every opportunity
to catch.

Harold's Chicken Shack #86

we're trying to eliminate the shack.
— Kristen Pierce, Harold's CEO
& daughter of founder Harold Pierce

when i went to summer camp the white kids had a tendency
to shorten names of important institutions. make Northwestern
University into *NU*. international relations into *IR*. everybody
started calling me *Nate*. before this i imagined myself

Nathaniel A. maybe even *N. Armstead* to big up my granddad.
i wrote my whole name on everything. eventually i started
unintentionally introducing myself as *Nate*. it never occurred
to me that they could escape the knowing of my name's
real length. as a shorty

most the kids in my neighborhood couldn't say my name.
Mick-daniel, Nick-thaniel, MacDonnel shot across the courts
like wild heaves toward the basket. the subconscious visual
of a chicken shack seems a poor fit for national expansion.

Harold's Chicken is easier, sounds like Columbus's flag stuck
into a cup of coleslaw. shack sounds too much like home
of poor people, like haven for weary,
                                    like building our own.

directions

go west homeboy.   274 toward the suburbs Daddy driving & you
at his side. bag in back.   *go west homeboy.*   the road
warm in front of you.   summer & bootleg sunglasses.
     go west homeboy.   his face from summer camp blurs
in your eye.   you exchanged numbers & a keep in touch but
you did not expect it.   *go west homeboy.*   at County

Line Road when you exit there's a building with a golden dome,

                    a bank or house
of prayer.   *go west homeboy.* turn into the neighborhood
          & search for the house.   a school-
     sized building has the address & Daddy pulls up around back.
go west homeboy.   the home is on a hill.
          the driveway leans you back like a rollercoaster.
     go west homeboy. the blur stands
at the top with his pops. pastel polos & the same faces smiling.
          go west.

off white

dark green in a city, on a building, might mean
a park district, a field house, that color is dull,
maybe its off-forest or semi-olive.

maybe in the field house there's a basketball
gym upstairs with crooked floorboards,
the smell of musk & mold & something

sort of green. the air tastes like chlorine
wafting from the pool downstairs.
i was there every week ready to play

or maybe ready to be played by coach
or referee. the beginning of each game
was an awkward pledge

to fairness maybe, something of that
sort but i can't recall. our team was
a different shade from the catholic

school boys we played.
maybe that was the allegiance or
the line the refs saw when

they called balls out of bounds
on the right side of the baseline.
or maybe that was the thought when

one boy smashed me over the head
with a heavy forearm. he was a mess
of freckles & brown hair clumped

sweaty into a cat-o'-nine-tails. maybe that
was blocking the referees' view.
something about those colors

all around & all a little wrong,
a little faded, or dull, or dark
or something like that.

juke

in dark basement they dance violent
in violet light like a fight or fuck.
boy against wall back bent like a bow
aiming an arrow. she is all knees,
thighs driving into him,
punching his center like a clock.
working & rotating.

she is sturdy ballet
on a single leg, her
homegirl holding her up.
he is playing man,
grabbing, thrusting
like beating, bass banging
into him & out again. he
is balancing on both feet.
tiptoes & swivel
in his new shoes;

       they gleam bright, 1 of the few
       sources of light, like she is,
       or the purple lamp in the corner
       nobody can see.

church in the wild

Tuesday's children
wait on the pavement for
the church doors to open
singing *the thong song.*

Tuesday's children
make popsicle stick statues
of jesus & other action figures,
like mama or grandma or play auntie.

Tuesday's children
sit in the sanctuary,
sing in the shake
of voice change.

Tuesday's children
see the first lady take a broomstick
to the back of her youngest
for being a bully

                  & other stories about rods.

Tuesday's children are the light
of the world turned on
to break up the basement party
right when it was getting live.

Tuesday's children are big
jeans tied up with twine
or short skirts made dress
by a virtuous t-shirt.
Tuesday's children are holy
as hell, praying for mercy,
on the lamb of God
with a grape juice chaser.

Chicago high school love letter

graduation

333.

hold me
before
i
disappear.

Note: the numbers in "Chicago high school
love letters" represent the city's homicides
during the 2007–2008 Chicago Public
Schools academic year.

picking flowers

Grandma's rosebush
reminiscent of a Vice Lord's do-rag.
the unfamiliar bloom in Mrs. Bradley's yard
banging a Gangster Disciple style blue.
the dandelions all over the park putting on
Latin King gold like the Chicano cats
over east before they turn into a puff
of smoke like all us colored boys.

picking dandelions will ruin your hands,
turn their smell into a bitter cologne.

a man carries flowers for 3 reasons:

> *• he is in love*
> *• he is in mourning*
> *• he is a flower salesman*

i'm on the express train passing stops
to a woman. maybe she's home.
i have a bouquet in my hand,
laid on 1 of my arms like a shotgun.
the color is brilliant, a gang war
wrapped & cut diagonal at the stems.
i am not a flower salesman.
that is the only thing i know.

undress

my 2 fingers in the middle
of your back stumble & discover.

a grab & release of pressure
as lace & metal loosen, fall.

somewhere my other hand wanders.
a clumsy sculptor, trying to carve away

the stubborn left side of a string,
a thick strand, something silky

& bikini cut or a cotton boy-short number.
that last push & tumble of cloth

down your leg. my mouth is fat
with a syllable i won't speak,

an exclaim of relief.
we equals now in nothing.

the only thing we possess in
is what we earn by sweat.

cut

low crouch, point into no-
where. there is no happiness
here, the seat of deceit. brother
pull you out; big brother keep you
in. you victim, you victor, you
ball for hitting or wall for not
moving. you vast immovable,
unhurting thing like those before.

this is cruel double Dutch.
this is all time & time
& go. hop in, sit & eat.
think as little as you can.
man-making take time.
you putting in your time.
tic & tic & tic
& bloodsucker & such.

recycling

it's your 1st year of college & you should be missing
home by now but mostly you don't. you read the
Chicago newspapers & call family on Sundays.
you pick up going to church at a place adjacent to the projects.

you're not from projects & the ones in Chicago seem worse
but there's comfort in being around plainspoken folk.
the church folk feed you & also cook you food.
you take African American studies classes & sleep
through Spanish & write poems at night. you
read the newspaper. you consider pledging a fraternity.

you go to parties to watch people. you don't miss home.
you call your ex girl a lot. you imagine her face across
the phone line. you stare at the scar
on her chin. it is shiny & smooth. you read
the newspaper. you text new girls mostly. you invite
them to play cards & bet clothes or take them to dinner

on your birthday so you don't spend it alone
or you share their extra-long twin beds or you just text them.
it's your 1st year of college & your nephew is tiny
& your niece is young enough to be happy & the world
is new & you are not going home for Thanksgiving.
you are in the South at a new friend's house.

you go to church with his family & to his old high school's
basketball game & to his malls & to his grandmother's house.
you did not make your team past 9th grade & never went to malls
much. your grandmother has been dead for 2 years now.
you read the newspaper. his family are nice people.
you do not miss home. you go back to school. you stop talking

to your ex girl. she has a new guy. you do not miss home.
you write poems. you read the newspaper. there are still more
kids dying. your 1st year of college & you should be missing
but you're still here. you write papers about black people
& voting & violence & families & that is the same
paper. you don't read the newspaper. you have finals to finish.

you go to church on Sunday with your new friend & you
talk to new girls & consider pledging. you have heard
the fraternities will haze you. you have heard about beating
but you are not from the projects & you are not in Chicago.
you stop reading the newspaper. you decide to kiss a girl
& mean it. you decide to pledge a fraternity. you should

have more information about the newspaper. & the girl.
& the fraternity. you should call home more. you don't
read newspapers or call. you are not from the projects or
Chicago. you do not miss home. or your ex girl.
or your newspaper. there are still more kids dying. you
convince your new friend to pledge the fraternity.

he worries about the hazing, the beatings.
you tell him this is opportunity. don't miss it.

repetition & repetition &

we are love.
we are 1.
baby we are wild.
& we ain't crazy,
crazy to keep forgetting.
we realize that its
amnesia until
& shame.
wild like amnesia,
wild until we are free.
baby we are hundreds.

until we decide we are not
we are limited to the hood.
to the edge of the city limits
we are close
until they close.
in the schools
until they close,
in the pubs
until they close,
on the airwaves,
we are live.
a break beat,
a percussive imperative.
we are a pattern,
amnesia & shame again.
a national shame
under our single body.
a pool of grief puddling,
a stare into the barrel,
a push out into open air,
ours is a long love song.

ACKNOWLEDGMENTS

Thank you to the editors and staffs of the following journals and anthologies in which the following poems have appeared (often in slightly different versions):

Anti-: "prelude"; *AREA Magazine*: "Mama says"; *Beloit Poetry Journal*: "Chicago high school love letters"; *The Collagist*: "church in the wild"; *Connotation Press: An Online Artifact*: "cut," "directions," "off white," "picking flowers"; *Day One Amazon Literary Subscription*: "out south"; *Heavy Feather Review*: "landing," "Indian summer," "in the land where whitefolk jog"; *The Incredible Sestina Anthology*: "pallbearers"; *Indiana Review*: "juke"; *The Journal*: "Granddaddy was the neighborhood," "1st love song to the black girl at smart camp"; *MisPoesias*: "repetition & repetition &," "Harold's Chicken Shack #1"; *Muzzle*: "god made the hundreds, man made it wild"; *Nashville Review*: "palindrome"; *New Republic*: "recycling"; *Poetry*: "praise song," "Harold's Chicken Shack #86"; *RHINO*: "buying new shoes"; *South Side Weekly*: "pronounce"; *Southern Humanities Review*: "niggaicouldhavebeen #1," "learning gang handshakes"; *Southern Indiana Review*: "when it comes back"; *pluck!*: "Fame Food & Liquor," "Ragtown prayer"; *[PANK] Magazine Online*: "Harold's Chicken Shack #35"; *Union Station Magazine*: "on being called a nigger in Ann Arbor, MI, on South University Street by a drunk ticket scalper."

The poem "Mama says" won the 2013 Gwendolyn Brooks Open Mic Award and was published on the website of The Guild Complex.

Many of these poems were included in a winning manuscript for a 2013 Hopwood Graduate Poetry Award from the University of Michigan.

Many of these poems appeared in the chapbook *Blood Percussion*, published by Button Poetry.

Special thanks go out to a number of readers, editors, friends, & supporters. This book would not have been possible without these folks & countless others.

Dark Noise: Aaron Samuels, Fatimah Asghar, Danez Smith, Jamila Woods, & Franny Choi. My family, my loves, my greatest allies.

My brothers: José Olivarez, Lamar J. Smith (JusLove), Shaun Peace, Demetrius Amparan, Ben Spacapan, Ben Alfaro, Chris Marve, Christian Nuñez, Bryson Whitney, & Jeremy Williams. You all have co-lived many of these poems.

My great writing friends & editors: Blue Bellinger, H. Melt, Raymond McDaniel, francine j. harris, Angel Nafis, Isaac Miller, Brittany Bennett, John F. Buckley, Joshua Bennett, Katy Richey, Morgan Parker, Caroline Randall Williams, Don Share, & Phillip B. Williams.

My teachers & mentors: Sandra Cap, Liz Graf, Kevin Coval, Idris Goodwin, Avery R. Young, Mark Jarman, Alice Randall, A. Van Jordan, Linda Gregerson, Laura Kasischke, Khaled Mattawa, & Keith Taylor.

Thanks to the institutions that have held, supported, & defended this work: The Cave Canem Foundation, The Hurston-Wright Foundation, Young Chicago Authors, Neutral Zone Literary Arts, Oklahoma Literary Arts Alliance, Vanderbilt University, & The Helen Zell Writers' Program at the University of Michigan.

My editor Ed Ochester & the team at University of Pittsburgh Press for selecting this book.

My students, particularly the 2014 YCA Guthman Interns, Alex Pan, & Carlina Duan.

My whole family for all the love, support, & swagger.

The cipher & all of the MCs I've built with over the years. You all were my first writing workshops.

All of Chicago, especially the South Side, especially the Hundreds, for being my best classroom & my heart.